www.finishinglinepress.com

Our Lady of Perpetual Loss

poems by

Shelley Jinks Johnson

Finishing Line Press
Georgetown, Kentucky

Our Lady of Perpetual Loss

Publisher: Leah Huete de Maines
Editor: Christen Kincaid
Cover Art: Morgan Lasyone
Author Photo: Abigail Blalock
Cover Design: Elizabeth Maines McCleavy

Order online: www.finishinglinepress.com
also available on amazon.com

Author inquiries and mail orders:
Finishing Line Press
PO Box 1626
Georgetown, Kentucky 40324
USA

Contents

For all those who have pierced the veil before me.
Love never dies.

Grief's Masquerade

King to my loneliness,
Queen to my pain.
I am the royalty
ruling all action.

My voice opened wide
screaming in vain.
I am the song
long out of fashion.

My scars burn right
in the sun of your flame.
I am the ice
chilling your passion.

Love dies long
nightly in shame.
I am the dream,
fatal distraction.

Lend me your eyes.
Wake with a name.
I am called Memory.
Dissatisfaction.

Memory Keepers

who will be my memory keeper
when days pass into years gone by

who will light the flame of love
after night burns out to dawning sky

who will be the cup bearer
when waters of life run dry

who will till the soil of hope
keeping fertile land for vines

and at the end of days, my love,
waiting on the edge of time

who will blacken sun's love glow
or sing our final lullaby?

I, Historian

Let me write your name
in my book of losses.
Bookend the dates,
your story complete.

Let me wander through gardens
of cypress mosses.
Life forged in love;
death without conceit.

Let me remember your light,
a love that burns within me.

Toteetum

Sometimes
it feels like death is stalking me.
Not yet coming for me, but always
reminding me he's there—waiting in the wings.
I feel him skulking in shadows cast from bright joy.
Crouching in crevices of life's connections.
Hiding in hints of love and affection that try
to bloom through hardened parts of my heart.
Biding his infinite time for the limits of my own.
Waiting.
Wanting.
Hungry for the ones I would keep close and treasure.
Greedy to own everything and my inability to stop him.
Impatient for my fealty in the face of his power.
Smug in the security of his dominion.
There is a question on the tip of my tongue.
The answer, I know, will not be enough.
Courage catches in my throat.
Stops there. Dies.
Silent God
bides his
time.

Lullaby

I am tired
fatigue of life
that will not subside
my heavy breath
rattles with longing
my eyes
autonomous from my will
would close at ease
but for the horror
before them
commanding
an audience
my mind
never quiet demands
a break
it never acquires
my limbs walk
as my tongue talks
and my ears
will not go deaf
all around me
the sun rises
the winds blow
and time tries
to forget

Pandora's Gift Rejected

Looking back at all the times of our youth.
Books, music, incendiaries, and revolutions.
Conversations lasting through the murkiness of midnight
bringing us arrogantly wiser into the hazy-edged dawn.

There seems to be a disconnect from then til now.
A soul of promise lost under drowning waves of whiskey.
There was a boy, abandoned then claimed. Loved.
Navigating a harsh world through a bitter lens.
Hope and success and happiness seemingly
always on the edge of eternity, out of reach.

Looking backwards down the linear path
of that life rushing towards destruction with every
betrayal, bankruptcy, boot-kick, or bloodthirsty grab
there is a boy at the beginning. A babe.
Point A, where bright hope shines in crystal blue eyes.
Potential tied up with gossamer ribbon into a bow
waiting for one touch of love to unfurl
all that goodness and set it free into the world.

(for Shannon)

D minor

If I could set my grief aside,
I would write about the beauty of spring.
Lilac crocus pushing through
soil and straw while roses dance
in March winds.

I would construct metaphors
of new life, green and symbolic.
Bees and butterflies feasting
on blooms heavy with pollen.

I would not cry for the winter
cold of loss, barren landscape, death
of love. Not *of* love, but of *my* love.

If I could clean my face of tears,
I would sing of sun rays splayed
out from dinosaur-shaped clouds
and the crisp squawk of baby birds
newly hatched on my back porch.

I would not idly stare at the errant weeds
spilling over once pristine garden edges
nor think of how ashes become dirt
to feed the cycle of life.

If I could forget how I once loved,
I would throw my arms open
and laugh in the rain.

Winter's Idle

The cold bareness of winter's idle
is something I never understood.
Not in any personal way.

I understood the necessity,
like enduring a 5-hour drive to the beach.
Something to get through to where you want to be.
A small, insignificant inconvenience
compared to the reward of the destination.

But the cold of loss,
the chill of loneliness,
the bone-weary ache of emptiness

These were not sacrifices demanded of me
before jewels of March buds
and April blooms presented
themselves for my pleasure.

I did not know the oak's grief
at shedding its hard-grown leaves,
shriveled from the sun's turning

Until my sacrifice of survival
taught me love's true cost.
The bitter cold of enduring
each new weary sunrise demanding
my attention and asking
                              What now?

Hope and Prey

Somewhere in the sky was written
a cloud that said *I love you.*
But as I squinted into the light trying

to focus each trace of letter by hand,
the sharp sting of tears hazed
my vision until all that was left hovering

was a lonely red-tail hawk
circling,
circling,

Searching for the prey he had long
hoped to find in the chaotic
brush below, but never could zero in on.

Meercats

Marinated in vodka and lies
they come with their
Baby
Sexy
Sweetheart
WYD shortspeak
as though at the merest whisper
I should fold to my knees
to deliver what they desire.
My compliance
my agreeability
my subservience
None of which I possess.
I find those roles no longer fit
though there have been times
I've tried them on.
Outgrown more than
my wedding dress
and last years running shoes
I realize my response requires
hesitation
before I take what I want
and leave a ghost of
disappointment in my wake.

Chimera

I wrote a love song
   just to watch it die
on the lips of someone
   I thought I knew

But all too soon
   illusions lie
telling us stories
   that never come true

Still, I choose to believe
   silver screen smiles
painting veils over
   reality blues

Even as joy fades
   with a sigh
and sunshine burns
   to darker hues

Dancing

—after Pablo Neruda

Forgetting is so long.
Slivers of memory drift away
like hazy tendrils of the mind.
Moments dissolve too quickly
to catch, escaping through
the sieve of our fingers.

Life is short.
I forget to pause, breathe deeply,
grip intensely our souls' exchange
in a moment of laughter, our
essence transferred in a single
tear shed together.

Tonight I can write the saddest lines
as I neglect the persistent tapping
of a reminder to remember
in morse code, or something
similar. A language forgotten,
blurred.

Love is so short though I have loved.
When now becomes past
and I open my ears to the story
unfolding in my peripheral vision,
I remember.
        I remember.

You were beautiful. But now
you are gone and life,
I am reminded, will end.
Memory and forgetting will resume
their dance.
        Until the lights go out.

        (for Dolly)

Savages

Forbidden corners
darkened by universal
anguish of disconnect
loneliness and neglect

Filled with twining
hopes of adrenaline
and co-mingled
pheromones

Waiting for the spike
the thrill
the kill
the spill

Until the drop
cycles conscience
back into the last-
call lights of
closing time.

Bloomless Summer

Winter seemed no colder
than the last few years.
Especially '21 when we saw back-to-back
ice storms and I thought
my palm trees had died.
Sheer exhaustion is a real thing.
Like when I slept for months after
losing myself to caretaker role
and aligning my rhythms
to hospital beeps and bloody needles.
It takes the body more than a season to recover.
My jasmine vine hasn't bloomed
since the wilting of last fall;
crape myrtles struggle to open any buds.
Ants still march, but slowly with their labors.
Summer heat, heavy and oppressive,
weighs down even the best intentions.

Life is waning
in my colorless backyard.

And I think,
Maybe spring will not come again.
But I know it will,
no matter who is not here to see it.

The Dip and Dive

Darting artfully from palm fronds
drooping from the weight of death,
the dance begins at dusk
and gracefully cycles until dawn.

Dipping to water's surface
for the daintiest drink
they climb and dine
on a delectable banquet of bugs
awaiting their destiny.

Summer's divine gambol,
a feasting foxtrot weaving
dips, dives, darts, and dashes
into a drama of exquisite existence.

The night envelops me
and lulls a complacent joy
almost forgotten.
Entranced and delighted
I am unable to look away.

For Tim

There's a half-cocked smile
that shows up in the blue-eyed
face of a two-year-old.
A love of music legacy
deep in the DNA of a genetic
code steeped in the tradition
of the Beatles and an unfulfilled
need for satisfaction.

On mornings when we would
run and drink coffee afterward
the laughter of two men
commingles in my memory,
stirs a longing for days gone by.
Concentric circles of lives lived
that emanate out to touch
far beyond my salt-seared vision
or my short, longing fingers can reach.

There are dates of a month
we mark but couldn't
forget if we tried.
The 6th steamrolls in
before we can remember
the old month has died, so
we kiss that cherubic face
like a prayer of gratitude.

Choice as a Daily Meditation

It's hard not to take Death personally.
Not to ask god why
not to feel a neon target on your back
not to curse and scream and rage.

It's hard to walk along the rim of despair.
To not allow your body to be drawn downward
to where your eyes inevitably go
to not give into the call of the abyss
to not be lured by the lie of relief in oblivion.

It's easy to give way to self-destruction.
To lull in the comfort of self-pity
to believe the lies of forgetting
or the hollow promises of forgiveness.

The true work of grief is allowing
the sun's warmth to color your cheeks
the laughter of a toddler to pierce your heart
the kindness of a friend to touch the darkest parts
and the joy of a single moment

       acknowledging eternity captured there.

Dark Art

In the shadows of dives,
bathroom stalls,
and cheap carpet
a convergence of indiscretions
assemble.
Highlights of euphoria
accented by undertones of regret
give shape to a new reality.
From grayscale to dark,
tonal depths of field
textured rich with emotion
too rough to the touch
of an unpracticed hand.

Another bare back
awaits its stripes.

Collateral Damage

Dark places, vague faces
slurred memory, speech blurred
like the color of whiskey still on my tongue.
Throwing hands, slashing plans,
losing track of all the things I'd done.

I would apologize, wring my eyes
for all the wrongs at play.
But in the end when you couldn't win
you just turned and walked away.

I can't blame you for trying to tame me.
But the parasite inside me,
when it chokes and derides me,
Casts a shadow that will never escape me.

So I slant my eyes from the guilt of my pride,
look away from your face as you search out an answer.
I can't give you my penance
for the sins that live in us,
and you can't save me from anger.

Mute

I swallowed my voice
somewhere between here and Little Rock.
The exact moment hazed by music
filling empty spaces between us
as banter shifted to argument. Like
a roadtrip soundtrack to our destruction.

My voice
mute as the mandevilla growing gracefully
on the back patio, violent red blooms defiantly
claiming space amongst a tangled vine
of hombre greens. A haven for lizards and bees.

Vital
to the ecosystem of my backyard,
and yet unable to communicate
its thirst in the drought of summer's heat.

Silently
I rest my head on your chest, listening
to the rhythm of your steady heart

Beating
the thrum-song of my life

Dying

Chasing Selene

The water, calm as glass
mirrored out before us.

A peach-colored sunset behind us
reflects off the marble surface.

Gathering wildlife congregate at water's edge,
uninterested in the noise and disturbance of our boat.

No fishing tonight.
Moon hunters we are for this night only.

Searching for a reminder of how small we are,
drifting in a cosmos

as we wait for something new
to crash into us.

Thrum Song

There are moments
etched in memory,
painted with detailed precision.
Like this hummingbird
with its iridescent existence
flitting from red mandevilla
to loaded white jasmine vine,
darting from flowing fountain
back to the sweetness of bloom.
I close my eyes and smell life,
green with wonder, fresh with dew;
and try to overwrite memory of you.
Blue lips, whites of eyes, convulsing
limbs. Two words shattering all color
from my glass house.

Brain tumor.

Breathing in, slowly measured, I focus
on the orange of late summer skies
and try,   and try,   and try
to replace frail, clammy fingers
that can no longer grip mine.
Marking the time on my watch
for hospice accuracy.

5:07pm

This life thrumming in my garden,
Would I catch it if I could?
Or let it fly away?
Grateful at least

to have seen it.

Homeless Romantic

There's an I love you
hanging on my lips
      with no place to call home.

Displaced since you left.
Silently I repeat it
      over and over and over.

Searching for a new belonging,
it lingers, floating
      without a place to light.

Without connection.
Unknown. Unrecognized.
      I do not offer it up

for fear of never getting it back.
There is no insurance, and so
      I keep it close.

Quiet, waiting. Until
I learn to give it to myself.
      Without punishment

or guilt. Or fear
that one day you'll return and
      want it back.

Green

Death is a messy mistress.
She's cold, calculating, ruthless.
And in the end, she wins.
Every time.

She bides her time waiting,
then swoops in with urgency.
She is greedy, demanding
everything

but what is not hers to take.
Like fresh, tender shoots of love
sprouted from seeds of memory.
Or genetics

of hazel eyes and auburn hair
prescribed and preserved by god.
Or science.

Death is selfish and powerful.
But she is no champion.
The vines of life still grow

       down the world.

Peace Offering

I cannot
reconcile myself to all that is lost.

My tears no longer count the passage of time.
My laughter does not sacrifice itself to guilt.

Instead

my sadness reaches out a gentle hand
and offers it to happiness

in a gesture of peace.

THANK YOU

My journey with grief and path of healing have been unexpected. I find myself in a place in my life that I did not set out for, but there is joy and contentment here. I have not traveled to this place on my own. A rather large and eclectic community has supported me, nudged me forward, and encouraged me along the way. My gratitude is boundless.

To my Poetry AEX community for showing up, for teaching me, for cheering me, and for continuing to challenge me.

To my Bad GNUS Poets (David Atwood, Jim Clinton, and Beverly Easterling) for letting me have a front-row seat to your greatness and for keeping me grounded and accountable.

To REDDEX, Bentley, and Cole for teaching me that sometimes you have to go through the carwash with the windows down.

To my family and friends for early Friday morning walks, all-night pajama parties, book club laughs, Tuesday evening runs, Wednesday night choir rehearsals, cramped-room band practice, video-chat therapy sessions, and coffee shop meetups. Your love and friendship sustain me.

Shelley Jinks Johnson is a poet, entrepreneur, performer, and author from Alexandria, Louisiana. With a background in business start-ups and brand building, her pursuits shifted to writing and performing poetry after losing her husband of 15 years to brain cancer. In 2022 she founded Poetry AEX and was a contributor at the prestigious Bread Loaf Writer's Conference in Vermont. Co-founder of the Bad Gnus Poets writing group, she has developed her craft through various workshops and submitting her work to critical peer review. Her poetry grapples with themes of death, acceptance, self-discovery, and how to find meaning in life after loss. She has discovered that living a life of creativity is the best way of building a life of value rooted in joy and gratitude. That discovery emboldens her to help others tap into their own creative wells, thereby enriching their lives and the broader community in which they live and thrive.

Her first collection of poetry *PRETTY LITTLE WIDOW* was published May 2023 and her debut children's book *NORTH STAR,* March 2024. *Shelleyjinksjohnson.com*

www.ingramcontent.com/pod-product-compliance
Lightning Source LLC
Chambersburg PA
CBHW022059080426
42734CB00009B/1417